EARTHWISE

Getting Around

Jim Pipe

Stargazer Books

CONTENTS

© Aladdin Books Ltd 2005

First published in the
United States in 2005 by:
Stargazer Books
c/o The Creative Company
123 South Broad Street
P.O. Box 227
Mankato
Minnesota 56002

Printed in U.A.E.

All rights reserved

Editor
Katie Harker

Educational Consultant
Jackie Holderness

Series Design
Flick, Book Design
and Graphics

Designer
Simon Morse

Picture Research
Brian Hunter Smart

Library of Congress
Cataloging-in-Publication Data

Pipe, Jim, 1966-
   Getting around / by Jim Pipe.
      p. cm.-- (Earthwise)
   Includes index.
   ISBN 1-932799-52-4 (alk paper)
   1. Travel--Juvenile literature.
   2. Transportation--Juvenile literature.
   I. Title. II. Series.

G175.P57 2004
388--dc22   2004042867

INTRODUCTION

Most of us make several journeys each day. We may walk to school, take the bus to the store, or travel in a car to visit friends. Maps and routes help us find our way. Sometimes, we make longer journeys using planes and trains. There are lots of different ways to get around!

HOW TO USE THIS BOOK

Watch for the symbol of the magnifying glass for tips and ideas on what to look for where you live.

The paintbrush boxes contain activities that relate to transportation in your local area.

JOURNEYS

How many journeys do you make in a week? Like many people today, you may move around a lot. Most towns are growing, so people live farther and farther from where they work or go to school. Families use buses or cars to go shopping. Travel has also become less expensive. Many people now fly long distances to go on vacation.

Where Do You Go?

Think about the different journeys your family makes:

- Shopping—to get things you need
- Daily travel—to get to school or work
- Special journeys—to visit family and friends, to go on vacation, to move house
- Emergencies—to go to a hospital

Write down how you would travel. When would you fly in a plane? When would you ride a bike?

School bus

Walking to local stores

Traffic is a word used to describe vehicles on the move, such as cars, bicycles, motor rickshaws (left), and buses.

When lots of people travel at the same time, it can cause traffic jams. If there are too many vehicles, everyone has to move very slowly.

TRANSPORT

Any vehicle that helps to move people or goods is a type of transport. What vehicles can you see in your area? In addition to cars and buses, perhaps some people still use animals to pull carts or sleds. If you live near a lake or the sea, watch for boats. Don't forget to look up for planes in the sky!

Dog sled

Boat

Most routes have signs that tell us which way to go and how far away places are. They help us work out how long a journey will take.

ROUTES

You may be going shopping or flying off on vacation, but every journey you take follows a route. Paths, sidewalks, streets, roads, and rivers all provide routes for us to follow.

Routes are important because when we start on a journey, we usually can't see the place we want to reach.

ON • THE • LEVEL

It is much easier to travel along a flat path than it is to climb up and down hills. That is why viaducts and cuttings are used to create a level route for cars or trains.

A viaduct is a bridge that crosses a valley (right). Cuttings are where hills have been cut away. Can you find any in your area?

The shortest route between two places is a straight line. We call this a direct route. However, hills, buildings, lakes, or the sea can get in the way. This forces the route to twist and bend. But tunnels and bridges can help a road to continue in a straight line.

The best route is not always the quickest or shortest. When you are vacation, for instance, you might take a route that has beautiful scenery. This is more relaxing than rushing along a highway where there is little to see.

Route Race

Set a route for your friends across school. See who can find the quickest route. Use a watch to time them. Then draw a map to show their different routes. Did the quickest route follow a straight line?

LANDMARKS

On short journeys, we can remember the route by looking for landmarks. These are objects on the landscape that are easily spotted. Landmarks can be natural features such as cliffs, lakes, and woods, or tall structures such as churches, mosques, and bridges. Even when we have a map, landmarks are helpful because they give us clues about where we are.

Eiffel Tower

Many cities have a particularly tall landmark that can be seen from far away. In Paris, you can see the Eiffel Tower for many miles. In San Francisco, the Golden Gate Bridge towers over the harbor entrance.

Tall buildings make good landmarks.

Golden Gate Bridge

Route Map

Think about a short journey that you know well, such as the route to a friend's house or your route to school. Make a list of landmarks you pass. You may want to draw your route, like this example (right). Remember to show landmarks and the places where you turn left or right or where you have to cross the road.

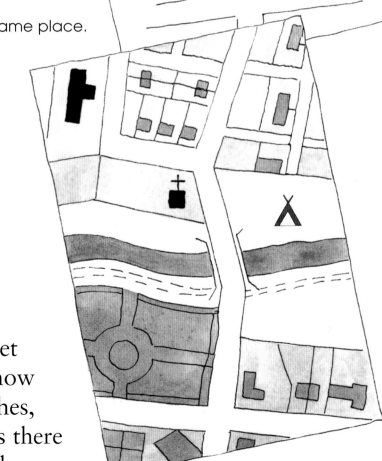

These maps show the same place.

Windmill   Highway   Zoo

Bridge   Picnic   Campsite

Airport   Wildlife park   Beach

Compare your route map with a street map of the same area. Street maps show landmarks, such as bridges and beaches, with symbols (above). On most maps there is a list telling you what these symbols mean.

MAPS

Maps help us find our way around places we don't know. Street maps show roads and buildings in a town, while walking maps show features such as hills, woods, and rivers. A tourist map points out interesting places to visit. World maps show all the continents, islands, and oceans of the world.

Route maps such as a road atlas help us to plan journeys. Important roads look the biggest.

C OMPASS

Wherever you are, a compass can tell you in which direction you are going. Line up the needle so that it is pointing to N for north. With the needle in this position, the letters E, S, and W point to east, south, and west. Using a compass and map together makes it easy to know exactly where you are!

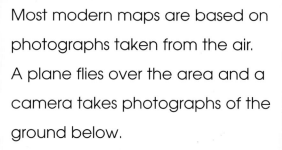

Most modern maps are based on photographs taken from the air. A plane flies over the area and a camera takes photographs of the ground below.

The photos are put together to give the mapmaker a view of the whole area. Today, maps are also made from pictures taken by satellites in space (main picture).

Walking Map

Walking maps show natural features such as cliffs as well as paths, roads, and buildings. Lines called contours show the height of the land. Where the lines are close together, the hill is steep. The next time you go for a walk in the country, use a map to follow your route. Look out for features such as rivers that can help you find your way.

Satellite photo of Los Angeles

Woods

Contour lines

Railroad cutting

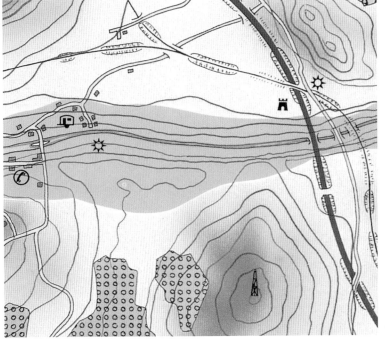

HOW DO I GET THERE?

Using maps, we can plan our route. Then we can decide how we want to travel. Today, there are lots of different ways of getting around.

On short trips you might walk, cycle, or take the bus. On longer journeys you might travel in a car or train, fly from an airport, or take a ferry.

Paint Your Journey

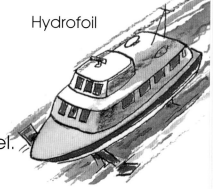

Hydrofoil

Many artists like to paint transport vehicles, such as ships or planes. Others like to paint the countryside when they travel. Paint your own picture of your favorite vehicle or journey.

Drawing lines behind a plane shows that it is moving!

Road

Motor vehicles such as cars, buses, and motorcycles are a handy way to get around. They can pick you up from your front door!

Air

Planes are the fastest way to travel. Many jetliners travel at around 550 mph. They can carry 500 people across the Atlantic Ocean in 5 hours.

Rail

Fast trains link large towns. Slower trains link places on the edge of a city, called suburbs, with the city center. One train can carry the same amount of people as 1,000 cars.

Sea

Ships cross oceans, providing links between continents. Ferries can carry 1,000 passengers and 400 cars across seas and lakes. Some have cabins for people to sleep in on long journeys.

A plane carries a package across the world.

A van brings it to your door!

MOVING GOODS

Transport also helps us to move heavy goods from one place to another. Factories need materials that come from different places around the world. A lot of the food that we eat is grown in other countries. Planes are used for small or urgent deliveries. Trucks, trains, and ships are better for moving heavy loads.

Be a Truck Driver

Write a story about what it is like to be a truck driver. First, you might pick up a container from a ship. Trucks can carry goods a long way, so you may drive for many hours. You can talk to other drivers using a CB radio. In a big truck, you may even sleep in a bed at the back of the cab!

Container ship

Truck

The journey from an oil field to a gas pump

After oil is pumped out of the ground, it travels along huge **pipelines** for part of its journey. The Trans-Alaska Pipeline crosses three mountain ranges and 300 rivers!

Ships called **tankers** transport the oil on water. The largest tankers can hold more than a million barrels of oil. Barges carry the oil on rivers.

The oil is pumped from the ship to a refinery, where the oil is made into gas for cars. Then **tankers** carry the gas to gas stations.

When we go to a gas station, the gas is pumped into our car's **gas tank** along a pipe.
The oil has come a very long way!

Trains can carry goods over very long distances. The world's longest railroad line is in Russia. It is 5,500 miles long!

Trains may pull around 2,500 tons of coal, wood, or building materials, the same amount as 100 big trucks. But because trains run on tracks, they cannot provide a door-to-door service.

LOCAL TRANSPORTATION

How do people move around in your area? In most parts of the world, people use buses on short trips. Many big cities also have a rail network, either above or under the ground. Trains also link city centers with areas farther out, called "suburbs." In less developed regions, people also use animals, such as horses and donkeys, to move goods about.

Tram

Underground train

In large cities, buses carry thousands of people each day. At a bus stop you can use a timetable to find out where a bus goes, when it will arrive, and how long the journey will take.

Network maps help us find our way around cities. Different colors show different routes. Using the map below, work out how to get from Greenfields to Cow Lane in the fewest stops.

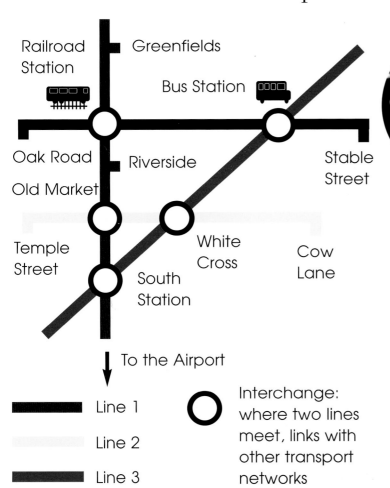

Railroad Station

Greenfields

Bus Station

Oak Road

Riverside

Stable Street

Old Market

Temple Street

White Cross

Cow Lane

South Station

To the Airport

▬▬▬ Line 1

Line 2

▬▬▬ Line 3

○ Interchange: where two lines meet, links with other transport networks

BIKEWAYS

In many towns there are routes for bicycles, called bikeways. Watch for any near you. They are marked by signs (below), or may be colored red or green.

Bikeways often keep cyclists away from busy car routes. They make cycling safer. But wherever you are cycling, you should always wear a helmet and bright clothing.

USING NETWORKS

Today, everyone relies on good transport links to deliver food and other goods to stores. Many people travel long distances to do business or to go on vacation. Most types of transport are linked by global (worldwide) networks. A network means lots of routes linked to each other.

Many parts of the world are linked by a system of long, fast roads, called highways or freeways (right).

The longest road system in the world is the Pan-American Highway. This connects the capitals of 17 countries in South America and is over 29,000 miles long!

Today, 500 million people a year travel around the world by air.

For thousands of years, traveling by road was slow, dangerous, and uncomfortable. When railroad networks were built 150 years ago, it suddenly became much easier to get around on land. In the last 50 years, flying has become a popular form of transportation.

Local network—bus/tram

Rail network

Air network

Sea network

How Networks Connect

On long journeys, people often use local networks that connect with bigger networks.

For instance, you might take a bus to your nearest train station, then catch a train to the airport. If you look at a timetable for each part of the journey, you can make sure that you have plenty of time to make your connections.

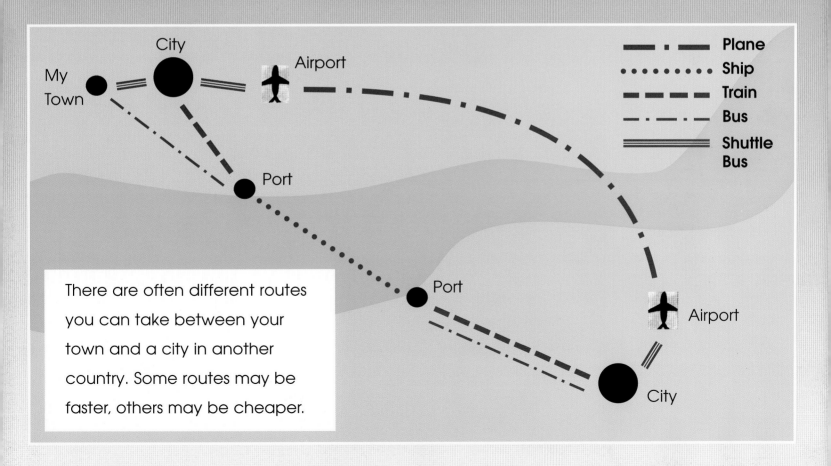

There are often different routes you can take between your town and a city in another country. Some routes may be faster, others may be cheaper.

Legend	
— · — · —	Plane
· · · · · · · · ·	Ship
— — — —	Train
— · — · —	Bus
═══════	Shuttle Bus

My Town · City · Airport · Port · Port · Airport · City

Ship ties up at port

MAKING IT WORK

Each transport network needs different things to make it work. Cars and trucks need good smooth roads and places to fill up with fuel. Trains need smooth tracks and railroad stations where people can get on and off. Planes need airports to take off and land. Ships need harbors where they can tie up and unload.

Passengers need to be looked after, too. Highway gas stations and ships have special areas for eating in (right), toilets, kiosks, and play areas for children. On trains, buses, and airplanes there is less room, so people usually sit in one place. Staff serve food and drinks from carts.

Like cars and ships, planes need to fill up with fuel before a long journey. The fuel is pumped into tanks under the wings.

All roads need regular repairs.

All vehicles need help to avoid other vehicles or potential hazards. Tugs help big ships to steer in narrow rivers and harbors.

Traffic lights and lanes help vehicles avoid each other where two roads meet. Lights also tell train drivers when to wait for trains coming from the other direction.

AIRPORT JOBS

If you visit an airport, watch out for all the different people at work in stores, customs or passport control, at ticket desks, or looking after the planes. Try to see the control tower. Here, air traffic controllers (right) let pilots know when it is their turn to take off or land.

TRANSPORT PROBLEMS

Bigger, faster transport networks help us move around more easily. But every type of transportation can cause problems. For example, cars are very convenient. They take us exactly where we want to go. However, cars also create lots of noise pollution. They also use large amounts of gas and oil and are expensive to make. The roads they use cut through the countryside (above), destroying natural habitats.

There are 400 million cars in the world today. The amount of traffic in towns and cities all over the world is growing rapidly. Although a lot of money is being spent on new roads, there are still traffic jams in many places.

NOISE POLLUTION

Cars, trains, and planes can make a lot of noise. As a result, living near an airport, a busy road, or a railroad line can be very annoying!

Smog is a mixture of smoke and fog. It makes the air look hazy. Smog is caused by fumes from cars and factories. In large cities, such as Athens, Greece, and Los Angeles (below), smog is a big problem in the summer months.

All over the world, cars and trucks are damaging the environment. The fumes from vehicles can lead to health problems, such as asthma and cancer. Fumes also build up in the atmosphere. They mix with water in the air, causing acid rain. When it falls, this damages trees and other plants. Jet planes also harm the environment. Because they fly so high, their fumes go straight into the atmosphere.

The weather can cause problems for vehicles. In fall, leaves on railroad lines can slow down trains. Fog and snow (above) can make driving dangerous. Storms can make travel dangerous for cars, planes, and ships.

MOVING FORWARD

Towns and cities are dealing with local transport problems in different ways. Many cities encourage drivers to travel into the center by bus or train. In some towns, cars must yield to pedestrians and the streets are safer for children. Other cities use tram lines to make travel easier in the city center.

TRAFFIC SURVEY

Study the traffic in your area with a friend and an adult. Which are the noisiest or busiest roads? Do heavy trucks create a lot of fumes? Are there places where children can cross the road safely?

Traffic Schemes

There is no easy answer to traffic problems. For example, if you improve the roads, they attract more cars! But traffic schemes can keep cars and trucks out of the city center. This can make it safer for pedestrians and will reduce pollution.

Trams

Amsterdam, Hong Kong, and Dublin all have tram systems to reduce traffic in the city center.

Park and Ride

In some cities, drivers are encouraged to park their cars on the edge of the city and travel downtown on a bus. Buses often have their own lanes and can travel quickly around the city.

Pedestrian areas

Many town centers have pedestrian areas. These are streets where vehicles cannot go.

Congestion charge

In London, England, drivers must pay a congestion charge if they want to drive in the city center. This aims to encourage drivers to use mass transit instead.

When cars park on the side of the street, it can make it hard for the traffic to flow quickly. So, on busy streets there are strict parking rules.

WORLDWIDE LINKS

Communications are all of the things that we use to keep in touch or pass on information. Communications include radios, TVs, telephones, and the internet. Good communications help companies to trade goods and services all over the world.

People are traveling more and more. Air routes link cities all over the world. But you are linked to the world in lots of other ways, too. You can find out what is happening in other countries from newspapers, the internet, or the television. More and more of the things you eat or items you use come from faraway places.

A big airport links places around the world.

Journey Search

If you are going on a long journey, such as a vacation, ask your parents or teacher to help you find out about your trip using the internet. You can find where you are going on a map. If you are flying, you can work out what places you will be flying over!

MADE • IN • CHINA?

Many objects have a label on them showing the country in which they were made. Do a survey of ten objects around your home or classroom. See if you can find out where they come from. Then locate these places on a map of the world or a globe (below).

Space shuttles already take astronauts into space. We also use satellites that circle the earth, bouncing TV programs or telephone calls to the other side of the world. In the future, there may be networks linking Earth with the moon or Mars!

HOW CAN WE HELP?

No one likes sitting in a traffic jam for hours. But everyone can help. The simplest way is for people to walk or cycle on short journeys.

On longer journeys it is better to use a bus or train rather than a car. A bus can carry 70 people, but often there are only one or two people in a car. So, using a bus creates less traffic, and less fumes.

R OAD • SAFETY

Car crashes kill 400,000 people around the world each year. Millions of minor accidents damage cars and cause traffic jams. But most accidents can be avoided if drivers follow the rules of the road and drive carefully. You can keep safe by sitting in the rear seat and wearing a seatbelt. On foot, always cross a street at a pedestrian crossing. Look in both directions before walking across.

Driving too fast can lead to a deadly accident.

Sharing a car

Taking the bus

Changing Our Ways

Here are some simple ideas for changing your family's travel habits:

- Do you really need to make that trip?
- Use a bicycle for short journeys.
- Walk to school with friends or a parent.
- Your parents can car pool with other parents to take you and your friends to school.
- Workers can also share rides to work.
- If possible, use a bus rather than a car.
- Avoid the rush hour.

A BIKE is a fun way to travel!

Poster Power

Many people enjoy driving their own cars. But how would you persuade them to change? Design a poster encouraging people to walk or cycle on short journeys, or to use public transportation. Mention the advantages. For example, cycling is good for your health and can be very relaxing.

USEFUL WORDS

communications—instruments that we use to exchange information, such as televisions, telephones, and the internet.

compass—an instrument used for finding direction, usually with a magnetized needle that points to magnetic north.

continent—one of the earth's large land masses, such as Africa or Asia.

contour—a line on a map or chart joining points of equal height or depth.

cutting—where hills have been cut away to build a road or railroad.

goods—products that are carried, usually by land, sea, air, or rail.

junction—interconnecting roads and bridges designed to prevent streams of traffic crossing one another.

landmark—a prominent or well-known object or feature of a particular landscape.

network—lots of routes linked to each other.

pedestrian—a person traveling on foot.

pollution—harmful or poisonous substances introduced into the environment.

route—the choice of roads used to get somewhere.

satellite—a device orbiting the earth, used to transmit information.

suburb—a residential district situated on the outskirts of a city or town.

traffic—vehicles on the move, such as cars, buses, and trucks.

viaduct—a bridge, usually for carrying a road or railroad across a valley.

Find Out More

Books:
Geography for Fun: People and Places (Stargazer Books); Look Inside Machines: Trains, Jetliners, Trucks (Stargazer Books)

Websites:
www.howstuffworks.com
www.ecokids.ca

PAST • TIMES

Look out for older types of transportation in your area or when you are on vacation. In some city centers you can still travel by horse and cart. In some towns you can also take a short ride on a steam railroad. If you live near a canal, see if you can find the long canal boats. If you live by the sea, look out for tall sailing ships.

INDEX

Photocredits

Abbreviations: l-left, r-right, b-bottom, t-top, c-center, m-middle

Front cover tl & br, back cover, 5brt, 6tl, 13tl, 14ml, 15tl, 15mtr, 17c, 21mr, 22tl, 22bl, 22-23, 23b, 25br, 26c, 26br, 27mt, 28tl, 29bl, 30mr — Photodisc. Front cover tr & bl, 2-3, 6br, 7, 8tr, 13tr, 13bl, 14tl, 14br, 16mr, 18 both, 19tl, 19c, 20tl, 20-21t, 21tr, 21br, 22br, 28b, 29mr, 30-31, 31bl — Digital Stock. Front cover inset, 3b, 4mr, 17br, 27mr, 29tr — Brand X Pictures. 1, 16b, 20br — Scania. 4tl, 5t, 19mt, 25tl — Flat Earth. 5brb — Jacquelyn Zettles/USCG. 4br, 12tl, 17tl, 20bm — PBD. 7tl, 15mtl, 16tr, 24br, 25bl, 30bl — Corel. 7br, 10-11, 19ml, 27bl — Corbis. 8bl, 8br — PhotoEssentials. 10c, 10bm, 13br, 24bl — Select Pictures. 14mr — USDA. 15tr — Comstock. 15br — Ken Hammond/USDA. 21bm — Eric A Clement/US Navy. 25tr — Brian Hunter Smart. 26tl — Digital Vision.